High-Sheriff
Jim Turner

HIGH-SHERIFF
JIM TURNER

High Times of a Florida Lawman

DAVID T. WARNER

RIVER CITY PUBLISHING
MONTGOMERY, ALABAMA

Published in the United States by Black Belt Press, an imprint of
River City Publishing
1719 Mulberry Street
Montgomery, AL 36106.

Designed by Lissa Monroe.
Printed in the United States of America

3 5 7 9 10 8 6 4 2

Warner, David T., 1948-
High-Sheriff Jim Turner : high times of a Florida lawman / David T. Warner.
    p. cm.
ISBN 1-57966-013-4
1. Turner, Jim, High-Sheriff—Fiction. 2. Sheriffs—Fiction. 3. Florida—
Fiction. I. Title.
PS3623.A8625H54 2004
813'.6—dc22

                            2004003441

To the "real" Jim Turner

With a special debt of gratitude to
Borden Deal and Linda Roe Dickinson
who helped with these stories.

Contents

Prologue:

Cousin Jim

Call him Jim, Jimmy, J.W., farmer, sheriff, raconteur. Sits on mossy banks of Suwanee River, rocking and observing.

Squirrels, hummingbirds, people. Amused, detached; yet, somehow involved. A kind man; none kinder. Yet a killer, too. Sender of two men to the electric chair at Raiford. Someone time forgot. A dinosaur, perhaps. An aging brontosaurus—an animal too noble to survive, breed, reproduce.

Yet a man, nonetheless. With a man's failings (occasional drunkard, player of poker in dark smoky boathouses). And privy to the failings of those around him (the politicians, the payoffs, the midnight trips in the skiff for more whiskey, women—floppy-breasted country girls).

The first time I heard his melodious country drawl was eighteen years ago when I was passing through Levy

County, Florida, on my way someplace else. A dime in the pay phone, and Jim's voice so like my brother's it's uncanny. (John must have picked it up as a child when he and my grandfather used to go hunting with Jim.) The voice makes me uncomfortable, reminds me of the home I fled, the obligations and responsibilities I dodged; childless and separated from kith and kin at thirty-one.

Still, I arrange a meeting. . . .

Fowler's Bluff on the Suwanee River—a community of less than a hundred souls. Jim comes to the door in his slippers. Stiff-jointed, frail, hawk-beaked, with pale blue eyes. My cousin, a link to my past. Leading me out on the back porch, he takes a seat on a rocker and motions for me to join him—grinning slyly like a tomcat with a dead bird.

Immediately, the good conversation. No preliminaries necessary. Man to man as contemporaries, though Jim's an old man. A mirror image of all that's good in me without the ruthlessness. An understanding and acceptance of people as they are. Not excusing, merely forgiving. Or if not forgiving, then accepting.

Never vain; seldom vengeful. And then only to right what's wrong. With Jim, there's always a reason behind his anger. A moral issue is involved.

Oh, you're a charmer, Jim; always, the charm. Turn it off and on like a spigot. Yet never a user; always a giver of something. Words. More than words. Wisdom.

Teller of tales. The voice understated. The gentle humor. Ironic, yet never biting. Stories involving governors, Negroes, whores, killers, friends and acquaintances. And always, the memory for names, details, dates. Who, where, when. Year, month, day, hour.

The long pregnant silences (me puffing on the cigarettes Jim is no longer allowed: "That cigarette sho' do smell good, David. I'm glad you're enjoying my cigarettes. 'Cause I sho' am enjoying watching you smoke 'em."). Both of us musing. Jim on the past, me on the future.

Tell me, Jim, was it any different when you were younger? Did you ever rage and gnash your teeth? Want to be senator, governor, president, anything besides yourself?

What's that, Jim? Say you're weak as owl shit?

Don't die, Jim. Be like one of those sea turtles that lives a thousand years. Lie on the beach and observe till you know all the answers. Then, tell me.

1

Levy County

Levy County is twelve hundred square miles of slash pine and sandy soil in northwest Florida. At its easternmost boundary sits the county seat of Bronson; at its westernmost—smack dab in the Gulf of Mexico—lies the tiny fishing village of Cedar Key. Fifteen thousand and forty-odd souls inhabit the county. Of which total, twelve percent are black; the remainder, white (with an occasional Greek or Cuban thrown in for seasoning).

The county was named after David Levy. Mr. Levy was Florida's first U.S. senator and the first Jew to serve in the United States Congress.

It was Levy who raised the money to build Florida's first cross-state railroad, which ran from

Fernandina on the Atlantic to Cedar Key on the Gulf. The railroad was completed around the time of the outbreak of the Civil War. As a result, miles of track at both ends were taken up by occupying Union forces. The remainder was confiscated by Confederate troops to replace that destroyed by Sherman's forces during his infamous march through Georgia.

But enough about Levy and his ill-fated railroad . .

Let's move on to my illustrious ancestor, James S. Turner. Turner arrived in Levy County in 1847 with a wagonload of calico for sale and wound up controlling most of the business interests hereabouts. (The family had somehow managed to blow it all by the time I arrived on the scene.) He was the first to ship Florida cattle out of Cedar Key on flat-bottom schooners to Cuba. And it was him who introduced Bermuda grass into Florida to serve as cheap fodder for those same cattle. Turner was paying a visit to Galveston when he come on a strain of grass folks thereabouts claimed would grow most anywheres—including the sandy soil of Florida. When Turner heard that, he scooped up some squares of the stuff, wrapped them up in newspaper so as not to damage the roots, and toted them home in a burlap sack.

I reckon you know the rest. If not, go anyplace in Florida and start walking. That stuff you're stepping on . . . that's Bermuda grass.

Moving up to more recent times, I reckon the most famous tourist ever to pass through Levy County was Mrs. Franklin Delano Roosevelt. Mrs. Roosevelt stopped by Simon Green's general store to Chiefland and bought herself a bottle of Coke and some soda crackers. Then, she got back in her chauffeured limousine and drove on off.

Me? My name is Jim Turner, and I was born and raised in these here parts. As was my Daddy before me, and his before him.

I was five times elected High-Sheriff of Levy County. During that time, it was my sad duty to kill two men. The first was caught in the act of raping his eight-year-old daughter. The second was a matter of self-defense. Or so I thought.

But enough about me . . .

The fact of the matter is, I love this county. Love every square inch of her, and all the inhabitants thereon. Some might not be what most people consider fine and upright citizens. But they are all of them human. And, in the long run, that's all that counts.

But I've been yakking your ear off long enough. I never claimed to be no politician, yet here I am jawing away like a Baptist sinner come Judgment Day.

Anyways, if you're ever down around Fowler's Bluff on the Suwanee River, drop by my house, and I'll tell you all you want to know. And more besides. Provided you remember to bring along a fifth of Canadian Club. (And, if you forget, there's a brand-spanking-new package store located just down the road to Chiefland.)

Only, you had better hurry. . . .

Most generally, the Suwanee River floods every ten years or so. Last time it flooded was in the spring of '77. Don't reckon I'll be here next time.

2

First Love

I'm eighty years old.

Sometimes, I wake up in the morning, and I can't quite believe it.

I want to spring out of bed like I was sixteen again, full of piss and vinegar. Only, now, it's ease my feet over the edge of the bed, then shift my weight onto both palms till, ever so slowly, I manage to raise myself.

One nice thing is, I've always enjoyed my life. Enjoy it even now it's almost over. Enjoyed farming, turpentining, being sheriff. Enjoyed hunting, fishing, drinking. Enjoyed other people's children, a few good women, waking up and going to bed.

Most of all, I enjoy my friends. Two of 'em was here only yesterday. A couple who grew up near me in Levyville. Knew Paula Dugan.

God, that was a long time ago. Paula Dugan; brown hair, almond eyes, a tiny wisp of a thing. Fifteen at the time, and me a year older. Our offspring would be approaching old age now, if there was an offspring.

Don't forget, Daddy was a doctor. It would have been easy for him to do an abortion. But I doubt it. Not Daddy. Not that he'd hold anything against some doctor who did, understand—just couldn't do it himself. A kinder man never lived. Never once sent out a bill. Never even kept books. Pay him when you see him, and if you hadn't any money, then livestock or produce would do.

Paula Dugan. I never gave up looking for her. Still looking. I loved her, I suppose. The way you love your first love and no other afterward. No obligation, just love. Pure and simple.

The first time we did it was in the back yard of her parents' house.

"Do you love me, Jim?" she asked when we'd finished.

" 'Course I do."

I meant it, too. Never loved anyone else so much, before or since. Married a schoolteacher when I was twenty-six, but that was different. That was a house, and days working, and buying things on time, till she drifted into alcoholism and died. And I hardly even think about her anymore.

But, like I said, Paula was different. Paula arrived at a time when love was something new, then vanished before we could grow used to one another. Living with someone, that's what kills love. Watching 'em get up in the morning and stumble into the bathroom. With Paula, there wasn't time enough for that.

Eventually, Paula became pregnant. She came to me in that way women have like it's no big thing, hardly matters, even; only you know it matters more than anything. She was going to have the baby, and that was that.

I wanted to get married, but I had to talk to Daddy first.

"Go to your father, then," said Paula. "But he'll never let you marry me."

It's funny about women. Sometimes, they know a thing before it happens. It's like they can read the future.

Daddy was forty then, forty years younger than I am now, but to a sixteen-year-old he was already an old man. We lived in a two-story wood frame house at Levyville. It'd been in our family for nearly a century then. My great-uncle built it a dozen or so years after he arrived in Levy County from Tifton, Georgia, with a wagonload of calico for sale. The house burned down eighteen years later in the winter of '41, the same year they moved the county seat twenty miles inland to Bronson and Levyville started on the road to becoming a ghost town.

When I got home that afternoon, Daddy was standing in front of the fireplace in the den. Mother was in town shopping.

"What is it, Jim?" he asked when he saw how nervous I was.

"It's about me and Paula."

"She in trouble?"

I nodded.

"Want to marry her, I suppose?"

I nodded, again. I was amazed at how well he seemed to be taking the news.

"You can't do it, boy," he said with a sad expression.

What did he expect me to do? Abandon her? I didn't want to marry her, wasn't even certain what it involved. But I had to.

"You don't understand. . . ."

"'Course, I do. You love her, right?"

Once again, I nodded.

"Well, love isn't enough. It don't pay the bills, so to speak. I could help you out in the beginning, sure, but you'd only grow to resent her in time, son. Believe me."

It was the first time I'd ever heard him mention love. It sounded strange coming from his lips. I knew he had feelings for Mother and myself, but it couldn't be anything like what I felt for Paula. I wanted him to understand that, tried to convince him of the truth of it.

Only, it was no use. He wouldn't give an inch on the issue, and all the while we were talking he had the same sad expression like he was attending the funeral of someone he loved more dearly than anyone in the world.

When I threatened to run away, he said he was packing me off to private school at Atlanta. Then, he sent me up to my room and told me to stay there till he said come down. I never could disobey that man. Never dared. Not that he would have beat me. He never once laid a hand on me. He was just the sort of man you couldn't bear to disappoint.

I went upstairs to my room.

Around five, Mother came home. I could hear them talking downstairs in the den. I eased open the door to my room and eavesdropped. Daddy was telling Mother he thought it would be a good idea if I went off to private school. Said I would get a better education that way. He didn't mention Paula. Mother was against it. She wanted me where she could keep an eye on me.

But once he convinced her it was for my own good, she conceded.

Why didn't I make a run for it? I could have easily dropped the twelve feet from my window to the ground. God knows, I'd done it plenty of times in the past. After all, it was my duty to marry Paula. Still, I couldn't disobey Daddy.

Sure, I'd done things he wouldn't have exactly approved. Like the time four of us boys chipped in a quarter apiece on a bottle of bootleg Canadian Club, then drank it sitting on the dock at Cedar Key. I'd had to force myself to be sick after that. Even then, I was wobbly-legged when I got home and hid upstairs in my room. But that was different. Daddy didn't give me a direct order not to drink that Canadian Club.

The next morning, Daddy called me into his den.

"Son, I'm sending you off a gentleman. If you turn out a son of a bitch, it's your own fault."

We shook hands. Then, he drove me in the Model T to Gainesville. From there, I rode the old Seaboard to Atlanta.

School was all right except for geometry class. I never could understand that stuff. I tried, but it was no use. The instructor was named Mr. Groggs. He died not long ago. I read the obituary in the alumni magazine and celebrated with a couple of shots of Canadian Club.

One morning, Mr. Groggs told the class anyone failing to comprehend the next day's lesson would be spanked with a ruler.

When I left class, I phoned Daddy long-distance and told him what Mr. Groggs had said. I told him I was trying my damndest, but couldn't catch on. Daddy said no stranger was going to beat his boy when he'd never done it himself, then instructed me to catch the next train home to begin Christmas break early. In the meantime, he'd straighten things out about Mr. Groggs.

The next day, Daddy met my train at Gainesville. I asked about Paula, but he claimed not to know anything about her. The lumber mill where Paula's daddy worked had shut down, and the family had moved. Daddy asked how school was, and I said,

fine, except for Mr. Groggs. He seemed satisfied with that, and we drove home.

The next morning, I walked over to where Paula had lived. The family occupying the house didn't know where they had moved to—or, maybe, Daddy had gotten to 'em first.

Anyway, Paula was gone. I couldn't believe it. I'd spent the last three months at school counting the days until I'd see her again. Nothing mattered but Paula. I was certain Daddy would change his mind about us being married once he saw his grandson. After all, it would have been his own flesh and blood.

All that morning, I wandered around town, asking everyone I saw if they knew where the Dugans had moved. No one did. It was like they had dropped off the face of the earth. Remember, this was the winter of '23 in Levy County, Florida. Twenty miles then was a great distance. A hundred miles, and you might as well have crossed the Atlantic. Daddy and I were the only people in the immediate vicinity who had been as far north as Atlanta even.

Around one, a crowd began to gather at the courthouse. I went over to see what all the excitement was about. Big Charlie Watson was standing on the broad front steps of the courthouse, the crowd gathered beneath him on the lawn.

Big Charlie was a rumrunner. He owned a boat called the *Hatteras* that ran whores and hootch from Havana. Nine years later, in '32, after I'd married, Charlie asked me to carry a load of bootleg whiskey to Valdosta, Georgia. I was earning fifty dollars a month at the time, working sixteen-hour days, seven days a week, in a lumber mill. I had a '31 Ford roadster with a rumble seat. I was to deliver the hootch to a hotel in Valdosta and drive home the same day. I wouldn't even have had to get out of the car. The bellhop would unload it for me.

Charlie was going to pay me two hundred dollars to make the run. I never wanted to do anything so badly in my life. But I couldn't. I never made a nickel on whiskey. Drank plenty of it, but never made a nickel. Sure wanted to though. Damn, I wanted to.

Big Charlie was telling the crowd what had happened to James Taylor's wife, Nan. A nigger named Henry Carter had slipped in the house and raped her. Nan, being seven months pregnant, had miscarried. When James found out, he fetched his cousin—Porter Wilson—and they went hunting for Carter.

A colored man from Otter Creek called "Lord God" was pulling boxes in a field of pines—cutting vees in the trunks of trees and hanging buckets to draw turpentine—when Porter and James surprised him. They counted three and opened fire. Lord God dropped dead. He didn't know them. They didn't know him. He wasn't doing a thing in the world but taking care of his job. Porter and James left the body lying there and continued their search for Carter.

They still hadn't come back, and the crowd was getting restless. Somebody suggested they go to Rosewood where the colored lived and beat some information on Carter's whereabouts out of the inhabitants. The crowd yelled their agreement, and the men went off to fetch their guns.

I ran to Daddy's office in town to tell him about Carter's raping James Taylor's wife. When I arrived, he was attending a pregnant girl. She was seated, fully clothed, on the edge of the examination table. He had his stethoscope against her belly and was listening to the heartbeat of the unborn child. When he saw how excited I was, he excused himself and led me into his office. He sat me down in a chair beside his rolltop desk and asked what was the matter. I told him.

When I finished, he said, "Run home and tell your mother what's happened. If Maria's there [Maria was the colored maid] tell her for God's sake to stay indoors, not to step outside for anything. Then report back to me."

"Will you be wanting your gun?" I asked.

"No," he said firmly.

"Aren't you going to Rosewood?"

I was disappointed in him. After all, Carter was a rapist! What's worse, he had done it to a white woman!

"I'm going to Rosewood. But I won't be needing a gun."

I ran home. Maria was setting the table when Mother told her what'd happened, and she began shaking so badly she spilled a bowl of soup on her maid's uniform. Mother wiped it off as best she could with a dishcloth, then led Maria upstairs to my room so she wouldn't be seen through the downstairs windows.

"Tell your father not to go out there," Mother called after me as I was leaving.

Daddy, with his black bag, was waiting outside his office when I arrived. I told him what Mother had said.

"Sometimes, it's necessary to disobey someone—even if you love them. So I'm going. You want to go with me?"

I remembered his commanding me to stay in my room when I told him about me and Paula. Now, so many years later, I wonder what my life would have been like had I disobeyed him. I never raised a child of my own, understand. Always wanted one, though. He'd be sixty-three years old now. An old man. My son.

"Yes sir," I said.

The Florida Railroad provided Daddy with a converted handcar, with a two-cylinder engine and a belt running to the rear axle, to make his rounds on. Full-throttle, it'd do about twenty miles an hour. In those days, the roads were such, it would've taken at least three hours in the Model T to reach Rosewood. By rail, it was no more than an hour.

When we got there, smoke was drifting toward us through the cedar trees. The crowd at the courthouse had commandeered an engine and a couple of boxcars and had beat us there by half an hour.

What had been Rosewood was now charred ruins! When none of the colored would talk—most likely, through sheer ignorance of the rapist's where-abouts—the white men of Levy County had set fire to their homes and shot them as they ran out! Men, women, and chillun. Didn't make no difference.

They were burying the bodies in long, shallow ditches when we arrived. I counted eighteen bodies in one ditch alone, piled up on top of one another like rag dolls with the sawdust leaking out. Only, instead of sawdust, it was blood, and intestines, and brains. The stench was horrible. I excused myself and went off in the woods to be sick.

Big Charlie Watson was back in there, puking his guts out. He told me how they'd questioned Carter's wife and kids and, when they professed to know nothing, killed them. After that, spurred on by the thought of no witnesses, killing the rest had been easy.

The next day, they found James Taylor and Porter Wilson lying dead in the woods behind Brandon's Hill. Presumably, it was Carter who shot them. The funny part was, they never found Carter. Like I said, a hundred miles in those days was like an ocean today. He could've simply moved up to Jacksonville, and no one would have been the wiser.

Years later, Nan Taylor—James's widow—married a series of old men for their social security and is still living, blind and legless, in a trailer no more than a mile from here.

When I got back to where they were burying the bodies, Daddy was fixing to leave.

"Everyone here is past help," he said like one in a trance.

We walked back to the tracks in the remaining daylight.

That evening, Daddy called me into the den.

"Son, try to forget about Paula Dugan. Hate me if you must, but I'm not going to let you marry her. Better you were one of those colored dead in a ditch than married with a child at sixteen."

"But—"

"Hush. Some things are better left undone. Like what happened this afternoon. Don't know what it is about people; just crazy to kill a nigger, I reckon."

He said those words on a December's eve, some sixty-three years ago. Sixteen years later, he died in the same bed where he'd been born, but it's like he's with me this very minute. You get older, you start talking to dead people.

Big Charlie Watson's boat—the *Hatteras*—sank in Havana harbor, the winter of '34, drowning twenty-five Cuban whores. Charlie, however, survived and lived long enough to become a deacon in the Long Pond Baptist Church.

As for my son, I'm still searching. Just the other day, some friends of mine who knew Paula as a child dropped in. They don't know what happened to the boy anymore than I do. . . . But some day . . . Maybe . . .

3

Croix de Guerre

That Chauncey was a sho' nuff character.

I remember the first time I ever laid eyes on him. That would have been in the fall of 1918. He and Daddy were setting out on the front porch, splitting a jug of 'shine, when I come home from school one afternoon.

"Jim, this here is your cousin Chauncey. Chauncey, meet Jim."

"Pleased to meet you, Jim."

Chauncey took hold of my hand and grinned that infectious grin of his.

"Chauncey here is a bona fide war hero," Daddy said. "Show him that medal of yours, Chauncey."

Chauncey took an oak-leaf-shaped medallion out of his coat pocket and held it out in his palm for me to examine.

"That there is the *Croix de Guerre*," explained Daddy. "Chauncey was a member of the Canadian Air Corps and brought down a dozen Hun planes "enduring" the Great War. Ain't that right, Chauncey?"

"It was closer to eight, Frank."

"Eight, twelve. What difference does it make? We're talking round figures here."

At that point, an anxious field hand whose wife was about to birth a baby come 'round, and Daddy followed him back to his house.

"Jim, that Daddy of yours is a holy Christian saint," allowed Chauncey when Daddy had gone. "Why, if he hadn't decided to move back here after Tulane Medical School, Levy County wouldn't have a doctor atall."

"What's patching up a few field hands and mill workers compared to gunning down German aces over France?"

Chauncey raised a finger to his lips.

"Hush now, Jim. . . . When you get older, you'll understand some better the difference between folks like your daddy and myself."

I was about to ask Chauncey what he meant when he stood up to leave. It was then I noticed the silver-knobbed cane he used to steady himself.

Reading my mind, Chauncey said, "Got shot down behind German lines. Had to spend nine months in a prisoner-of-war camp."

"What was it like?"

"Weren't so bad. The food was tolerable, and I didn't have to worry about being kilt every morning. Here . . ." He handed over the medal. "I'm entrusting this to you for safekeeping."

"But . . ."

"But, nothing. I'd only misplace it if I kept her."

Several months passed without us seeing Chauncey. Then, one afternoon, he drove up in a brand-spanking-new Model T Ford.

"Strike it rich, Chauncey?" asked Daddy when they had done greeting one another and were seated on the front porch.

"In a manner of speaking. I'm working for Ed Circle."

Years later, when I was sheriffing, I ran into the fellow in charge of procuring timber land for Mr. Circle. He was the only man I ever knew could write a check for a million dollars on another man! A million and one dollars, and he'd have to get permission. But up to a million, that was all right. . . .

Daddy let out a long, low whistle.

"How did you manage to wangle a job working for him?"

"Just lucky I guess. Mr. Circle's business depends on state and federal contracts, so I'll be entertaining a lot of high muckety-mucks in the government. Which reminds me. You still own that fish camp on the Suwanee River?"

Daddy nodded.

"What say I rent it on a monthly basis? There'll be right smart of change in it for you."

"Well, I don't know about that. . . . Jim and I been spending an awful lot of time out there lately."

"This here won't cut into that none. Doubt we'll be using her more than two, three days a month."

"In that case, I don't see why not."

"Let's you and me head out to the camp and go fishing," said Daddy one fine spring afternoon.

Things were quiet when we arrived at the cabin.

Daddy pounded on the splintered wooden door.

"Open up, Chauncey."

Silence . . .

Daddy swung open the door, and we went inside. The smell of stale bourbon and cigar smoke hung heavy in the air. In one corner was a table littered with playing cards and poker chips.

"Chauncey, it's me, Frank."

Again, silence . . .

"Wait here, Jim."

Daddy headed toward the bedroom. He had scarcely opened the door when a woman's scream pierced the quiet.

"Who the hell are you?" demanded a gruff male voice from inside the room.

"The fellow that owns that bed you're laying on. Where's Chauncey?"

"Gone to town for supplies."

"Well, tell him Frank Turner was here, and I need to talk at him alone."

"Whatever you say, Hoss."

An hour or so later, Chauncey showed up at the house with a sheepish look on his face.

"Hear you paid a visit to the camp this morning, Frank."

"You heared right." Then, to me: "Jim, there's kindling out back needs chopping."

"But . . ."

"No 'buts' about it. Run along now."

By the time I was done, Chauncey had left.

"Reckon we'll be doing some fishing this spring after all," said Daddy.

Several years passed during which Chauncey's legend loomed ever larger on the horizon. His living quarters occupied the top floor of a Miami Beach hotel, and it was there he entertained the likes of William Jennings Bryant and President Harding.

"That Chauncey always was a handsome rascal," said Daddy when he seen me studying a photograph of him on the society page of the *Gainesville Sun*.

"What do you reckon it's like mixing in society like that?"

"Why not ask Chauncey hisself? He'll be visiting next week."

"Think he'll be wanting his medal back?"

"Mark my words, son. That there medal is the last thing on Chauncey's mind."

But Chauncey never showed.

"What do you reckon held him up?" I asked Daddy.

"Something of world-shaking importance most likely. In other words, something to do with money, a woman, or a combination of the two."

In the winter of '29, there was a photograph of Chauncey shaking hands with Al Capone splashed across the front page of the paper.

I showed the picture to Daddy.

"Reckon Chauncey's in with the mob?"

"No more'n anyone else runs in those circles. Hell, nowadays, with Prohibition going on, gangsters are like movie stars. Out to give the public what they want. There's a whole 'nother world out there, son. And the rules that governs us homefolks don't necessarily apply to the likes of Chauncey."

"You ain't just making excuses for him, are you, Daddy?"

"No sir, I'm not making excuses. I'm making allowances. When you get older, you'll understand the difference."

There was talk of Chauncey's running for governor in '32. Then, a story in the St. Pete *Times* claimed he had paid bribes to certain state legislators to obtain state contracts for Ed Circle's business interests.

Though the charges were never proved, the scandal put him out of the running.

"Reckon this here will ruin Chauncey politically?" I asked Daddy.

"I doubt it, son. The public has a short memory where politicians are concerned."

Sure enough, four years later, Chauncey ran for governor and won. On the afternoon of the swearing-in ceremony, Daddy lay dying on the bed where he had been birthed.

"Run fetch Chauncey's *Croix de Guerre*," he told me.

When I returned with the medal, Daddy took it out of my hand and held it up to the light.

"Right purty, ain't it, son?" Then, following a long, labored pause: "A medal like this weren't meant for the likes of a cracker like me. Naw sir, a medal like this was designed with Chauncey in mind."

"Why do you reckon they never made mention of his being awarded the *Croix de Guerre* "enduring" the gubernatorial campaign?"

"Maybe Chauncey didn't want to run on his war record. Then, again, maybe it wasn't his medal."

Those were Daddy's last words. He died that evening.

The graveside service at the Antioch cemetery had scarcely commenced when a chauffeured limousine pulled up and Chauncey got out of the back seat.

When the service was over and everyone had done paying their respects, Chauncey come over and said, "Reckon you know, without my having to say it, that your Daddy was one fine man. Possibly, the finest man I ever knew."

"He thought the world of you, too, Chauncey. His last request was to have another gander at that medal of yours."

"That piece of junk! Hell, Jim, I won that off a drunken RAF officer in a poker game. I never even made it to France. Got shot in the backside by a jealous Canadian husband."

"Wasn't none of your story true then? What caused you to make her up?"

"I knew it would please your Daddy considerable if he thought someone in the family had done his bit to make the world safe for democracy. But, now that he's passed on, I might as well own up to the truth."

"He knowed it, anyways."

I told Chauncey what Daddy's last words had been.

"Don't surprise me the least little bit. Frank Turner was the onliest man in the world who knew me for the scoundrel I am and loved me, anyway."

4

Greeks

The Greeks, you say . . .

That was in the winter of '35. I had been married for a couple of years and was working in a lumber mill—twelve-, fourteen-hour days, six days a week. The pay was fifty dollars a month, and I was sure glad to get it. Remember, this was "enduring" the Great Depression.

My wife's name was Martha. We had a '31 Ford roadster—with twin running boards and a rumble seat—I had bought off a fellow for two hundred dollars. Sundays, after church, I would drive to Cedar Key to go clamming. I kept a wooden skiff tied to a log piling in back of the fish house. I used to pole across the flats to a mud bank to dig for clams. One Sunday, a storm blew up, and I went in early. When I got back to the dock, some of the boys were in the fish house drinking moonshine. I joined them, and we were all near about drunk when there come a knock on the door. I raised up and opened it a crack.

Standing outside on the wooden stoop was Rose Watson. Rose couldn't have been more than seventeen, but you would never have guessed it to look at her. She had the "built" of a growed-up woman.

"That your roadster out front?"

I nodded.

"Reckon you could take me for a spin in her?"

"Sure thing," says I, not wanting the boys in back to get the idea I was henpecked.

I followed Rose out to the car. We got in and drove off. It soon became apparent she was after more than a car ride.

"But I'm married."

"So what if you are?"

Well, you know how it is after a fellow's been married awhile. He likes the wife well enough, but it's hard for him to turn down a little "strange," 'specially when it's throwed up in his face thataway. It ain't the wife's fault. It's just the way he's built.

I parked the roadster alongside a deserted road, and Rose finished up what she started. When we were done, she slipped back into her clothes, and told me to drive her to town. Back at the fish house, she got out of the car and, without so much as a word, headed off toward home.

When I went back in for another drink, the boys wanted to know what happened.

"Nothing. She wanted a ride. That's all."

They all pretended to believe me—everyone, that is, except Tom Gilchrist. He waited until I was leaving, then followed me out the door.

"What really happened, Brother Jim?"

"Nothing, I tell you!"

But Tom knew better.

"You can't fool me. About a month ago, the same thing happened to me as happened to you this afternoon."

"Really?"

Tom nodded.

"What you reckon her daddy would do if he was to find out about us and his daughter?"

"Kill us, most likely."

Rose's father, Big Charlie Watson, was a bootlegger turned lawman. Up until the year before, he owned a boat—the *Hatteras*—which ran whores and hootch from Havana, Cuba, to Ybor City at Tampa. Then the *Hatteras* sank in Havana harbor, drowning Charlie's mate, along with twenty-five Cuban whores.

Following that, Charlie got religion and used his influence to have himself appointed chief of police at Cedar Key. Like many another outlaw before him, Charlie took being a lawman serious. During his first year as chief of police, he established a sort of record by killing two men. The first was beating his wife when Charlie sent him to meet his Maker with a single blast from a shotgun. The second was cooking up a batch of moonshine when Charlie surprised him in the woods behind Brandon's Hill. Rumor had it the man was unarmed, but no one disputed Charlie's word when he claimed self-defense.

"That Rose, she's the light of Charlie's life," said Tom.

"Don't I know it!"

Charlie had been a widower for going on twelve years. Every Sunday morning, he and Rose would attend the service at the Long Pond Baptist Church. (If it hadn't been for Charlie, there wouldn't be any church since it was him who donated the money to have it built.) Rose would be all gussied up in her Sunday finest Charlie purchased for her at Tampa, and Charlie's huge bulk would be squeezed into a shiny-new, store-bought suit. "Morning, Charlie . . . Rose," the preacher would greet them. "Morning, Reverend," a beaming Charlie would reply. Then, taking hold of Rose's arm, he would allow himself to be led down the aisle like a groom being led to slaughter.

"I best be getting home now," said Tom. "The ole lady, she's fretful as a coon hound if I'm even a minute late for supper."

One evening, a couple of months later, Martha come home from shopping, and told me about a big commotion to Cedar Key. Seems Big Charlie Watson had caught four Greeks messing around with Rose and hauled them off to jail.

In those days, Greek sponge fishermen out of Tarpon Springs would dock their boats at Cedar Key after having spent months at sea. They generally had plenty of folding cash in their pockets, having sold their haul, and only two things on their minds—getting drunk and getting laid. Naturally, folks hereabouts didn't much cotton to them. For one thing, they were foreigners, but their main objection was to the all-fired horniness of the bastards. It was rumored a Greek would screw anything, including another Greek. Still their money spent good as the next fellow's, and folks couldn't afford to be choosy "enduring" the Great Depression.

"Who would ever have thought it of Rose?" exclaimed Martha. "Why she's scarcely more than a child."

Naturally, I didn't bother to disabuse her of the notion. "Let sleeping dogs lie" has always been my motto where women are concerned. But I couldn't help feeling sorry for those Greeks. After all, it could just as well have been Tom or me in their place.

The next morning, word was out around town the jail had burned down the night before, killing all four Greeks. It might have been an accident, I reckoned, but knowing Charlie, I didn't think so.

After work, I drove over to Daddy's office at Bronson. He was the only doctor in the entire of Levy County, and it was him who would sit as coroner in the case of the four Greeks. He was busy with a patient when I arrived, but after awhile he called me in his office.

"What's ailing you, son?" he asked when he seen the expression on my face.

"It's about them Greeks. . . . I know for a fact they didn't force Rose Watson to do anything she didn't already have it on her mind to do."

Daddy nodded.

"I figured as much. But what makes you so certain?"

It was rough going, but I somehow managed to tell him about Rose and Tom and me.

When I finished, Daddy said, "Those Greeks were murdered for doing what you and Tom done. Kind of ridiculous, ain't it?"

"Murdered, you say?"

Daddy nodded.

"When I examined them, there wasn't a trace of smoke in any of their lungs. What does that indicate to you?"

"That they were all four pretty much dead before Charlie set the jail afire?"

"Exactly."

"You aim to testify to that at the trial?"

"I do."

I pondered on that awhile.

"What d'ya reckon will become of Rose if her Daddy's sent off to the pen?"

Daddy shrugged his shoulders and sighed, "God only knows. . . . But one thing's certain. . . ."

"What's that?"

"Whatever she does, she'll have plenty of money to do it with. No telling how much money Charlie has managed to hoard away over the years."

Well, I reckon you know the rest of the story. About how Daddy testified at the trial, and Charlie wound up sentenced to life at Raiford. It was splashed all over the front pages of the papers at the time, not to mention the two or three times it was writ up in *True Detective.*

What you don't know is the story behind the story, so to speak. 'Cause I'm the only one who does.

Twenty years passed, and I was serving as High-Sheriff of Levy County. One afternoon, I was setting in the office when a lady from Otter Creek called and said her husband was fixing to rape their eight-year-old daughter. I got in the patrol car and drove over. Sure enough, when I arrived, the suspect, Harris, was astride his daughter on the bedroom floor. I separated them and hauled Harris back to jail at Bronson.

Later, Mrs. Harris testified her husband had raped their three older daughters in the same fashion. I attempted to keep a lid on things, but somehow the *Gainesville Sun* got wind of the case. Next, it was the *Florida Times Union*. Pretty soon, reporters from across the state were descending like locusts on Bronson. There was fixing to be a big court trial with the little girl scheduled to testify against her daddy.

"It'd be nice if you was to save the state the expense of a trial by killing yourself," I said to the suspect one noon. " 'Specially with that little gal of yourn scheduled to testify."

"You'll not get rid of me that easy, Sheriff Jim. After all, ain't as if I kilt her or anythin'. Could be she was enjoying herself."

It was then I determined to eliminate Harris myself.

That night, when I was alone with the suspect, I took a cattle prod in his cell, and poked him in the ribs with it. Harris landed hard on the concrete floor, and I finished him off with a kick to the head. After I made sure he was dead, I phoned an ambulance. When it arrived, I informed the orderlies Harris had died as a result of a fall from the upper bunk. Nobody bothered to dispute my word, and the cause of death was officially listed as accidental.

A month or so after the "accident," I was delivering a prisoner to Raiford when I decided to pay Charlie Watson a visit. Watson was in his early sixties by then—a lean, taciturn man who was dying of cancer. He had been following the Harris case in the papers and wanted to hear all about it.

When I had done relating the official version, Charlie looked me straight in the eye and said, "You kilt him, didn't you, Jim?"

Naturally, I denied it.

"You never could lie worth a damn. I only wish you'd been sheriff at the time I stood trial. Between the two of us we coulda saved the state a whole lotta expense."

"What d'ya mean?"

"C'mon now, Jim. Why'd you reckon I took such an interest in the Harris case?"

Suddenly, it dawned on me what Charlie was talking about.

"You mean you and Rose . . ."

"That's right."

I looked Charlie over for seemingly the first time. He didn't look much different from anyone else as far as I could tell. But then, neither had Harris. At any rate, I didn't push the matter. It was no good punishing him any further. 'Peared to me like he had been punished enough.

I left Charlie alone in his cell and drove on home. A month or so later, I read in the paper where he had died.

Another thirty years has passed, and Rose Watson is living in a run-down trailer no more than a mile from here. Rumor has it, following the trial, she headed down to Ybor City where she blew her father's savings on riotous living before turning pro herself.

Sometimes, when I think back on all that's happened, it don't hardly seem real. To this day the Greeks avoid Cedar Key like the plague. And Rose Watson? Well, she's deaf and toothless, the sort of addled old lady who will tell you her life story at the drop of a hat.

5

The Camera

I was thumbing through some old photographs the other day when I come across one of Tom Gilchrist and me. It must have been taken at a church picnic because some charter members of the Long Pond Baptist Church are pitching horseshoes in the background. If I recollect aright, it was my wife—Martha—who snapped that photo. Using a brand-spanking-new camera Tom had bought out of a Sears, Roebuck catalogue. Which puts me in mind of a story. But, let me start at the beginning. . . .

Tom and I grew up together in Bronson. My Daddy was a doctor; Tom's worked for the railroad. Mr. Gilchrist was a big, bluff, red-faced widower who had been known to take a drink on occasion. Most any occasion.

Once, Mr. Gilchrist was on a tear to Jacksonville when he spied a camera in a department store window. Without troubling over the price, he went in and bought her.

"What's that?" Tom asked when Mr. Gilchrist entered the house with the camera.

"A picture-taking box."

"How does it work?"

"Stand back, and I'll show you."

Tom stood back against the wall, and Mr. Gilchrist snapped his picture.

When Tom seen the developed photograph, he was fit to be tied.

"Reckon I'll ever have enough money to buy me a picture-taking box?"

"Here, take this one."

Mr. Gilchrist handed over the camera.

"The way I see it: a thing belongs to the person what wants it most."

After that, you couldn't wander far in Levy County without bumping into Tom taking a picture of something or other.

"If a fella didn't know any better, he'd think you and that there camera were of a piece," I told him once.

"He wouldn't be far wrong neither, Brother Jim. Taking a photograph is akin to playing God. It's freezing a moment in time for all of eternity."

Only, time wouldn't stay froze where Tom's daddy was concerned. When Mr. Gilchrist turned fifty, Daddy warned him he had less than a year to live if he didn't stop drinking. Mr. Gilchrist ignored Daddy's advice and was dead inside six months.

Tom took his daddy's dying hard. He quit work as a fishing guide and begun drinking full time at the jooks to Cedar Key.

One afternoon, I was at Brown's Fish House when I spotted him staggering down the road with his camera strung about his neck.

"Mind you don't drop that there camera, Tom!" I hollered after him.

Tom turned to face me, swaying something fierce.

"That you, Brother Jim?" he slurred, squinting up his eyes against the harsh glare of the noonday sun.

"None other."

Tom took a photograph of his daddy out of his jacket pocket and shoved it under my nose.

"He was one fine gentleman, weren't he, Brother Jim?"

"He were that."

"Least, I'll have this to remember him by." Then: "Come on along to the Sundance now, and let me snap your picture."

Only, the Sundance was closed when we got there. So I bought a jar of 'shine off a bootlegger who lived nearby, and Tom took my picture standing next to the Oyster Point bridge.

"Hear tell you're getting married," said Tom when the jar was half done. "Congratulations."

"That reminds me . . . I been meaning to ask if you'd serve as my best man."

"Are you sure you want me, Brother Jim? There must be any number of others who could do a better job."

"Course, I'm sure. You're my bestest friend, ain't you?"

By the day of the wedding, Tom was straightened out to where he refused a drink prior to the ceremony.

"Sure you won't join me for just one?" I asked, tossing back a shot of store-bought whiskey.

"No, thank you, Brother Jim. I'm not one of those fellows what can take it or leave it alone 'cording to the circumstances. I'm like my daddy. One drink is too many, and twenty ain't nearly enough."

Naturally, I didn't pressure him none after that, and we managed to get through the ceremony without stepping on one anothers' toes or otherwise disgracing ourselves.

After that, Tom would drop by our house once or twice a week for dinner. When the dinner things had been cleared away, the three of us would sit around the table and play Patience. Tom was a tolerable good card player and, most generally, he would wind up a dollar or two richer by the time the game was done.

One evening, after Tom had left, Martha said, "What that man needs is a good woman to look after him, and I've got just the candidate."

Sure enough, the next time Tom come to call, Martha invited Susan Higgins over to make it a foursome. Susan was a quiet, religious gal. And, at first, she and Tom didn't hit it off too well. Especially, since Susan didn't play cards.

Then, in the midst of narrating one of his thigh slappers, Tom come to a dead halt in mid-sentence and said, "Pardon me, Miss Susan, but I was fixing to let loose with a swear word."

"What do you reckon come over Tom this evening?" I asked Martha after they had left.

"Could be he's found himself a wife."

"Susan Higgins! She's way too churchy for Tom."

"A fella like Tom wants a body that'll look after him and see he doesn't get in trouble. And 'pears to me like Susan is just what the doctor ordered."

I figured then it would only be a matter of time before Susan got the hook through Tom's nose and commenced leading him about the pasture.

And I figured right. 'Cause the next thing I knowed Tom and I were standing alongside one another in the Long Pond Baptist Church, with Tom reciting his "I do's."

We didn't see much of Tom after that, and I was beginning to wonder what had happened to him when he showed up at our front door one evening trembling like a leaf.

"What's the matter?" I asked.

Then, I caught a whiff of his breath.

"C'mon inside. Martha's off visiting her folks."

Tom took a bottle out of his jacket pocket, and I poured two glasses half full of Canadian Club.

Tom downed his at a gulp and said, "I swear 'fore God, Jim, that there woman is fixing to church me to death. Ever blessed evening, it's another church service. I had reckoned Wednesdays and Sundays would be enough. But ain't that way atall. Mondays, it's the Baptist Men's League. Tuesdays, it's the Women's League. Thursdays, it's coffee to the preacher's house. Fridays, it's Vespers. It's gotten to where Saturdays are my onliest day of rest. But, even then, some old biddies from the church are liable to drop by unannounced.

'Cording to the Bible, even the Good Lord got hisself one day off a week."

"I reckon the Good Lord weren't a Hardshell Baptist!"

Tom like to bust a gut laughing.

"The worst part is Susan objects to my taking pictures. Claims a camera is the devil's own plaything."

"What put that notion in her head?"

"The commandment what says 'Thou shalt hold no graven image afore me.' I swear 'fore God, Jim, she's like one of them heathens what thinks having their picture took is going to steal their soul away."

" 'Pears to me that Susan is a mite over-pious."

" 'Over-pious' ain't the half of it, Brother Jim! That woman is a holy Christian saint! She don't smoke or drink or cuss. Or hold with them what does."

The next morning, Tom was up and gone before I even rubbed my eyes good. That man must have the constitution of his daddy, I thought, as I rousted myself out of bed and proceeded to pour cold water over my aching head.

When I come home from work that evening, Martha had a worried look on her face.

"Tom Gilchrist has disappeared, and Susan has the law out looking for him."

I told her about the night before.

"I figured as much. Where do you suppose he's run off to?"

"Most likely, he's got hisself a bottle and is holed up in the woods somewheres. Leave him alone, and he'll be home directly with his tail tucked neatly 'twixt his legs."

Sure enough, Tom returned home two days later. And Susan—Christian lady that she was—was willing to forgive him.

The next time we seen the Gilchrists was at a church picnic.

"Looky here what I got, Brother Jim," said Tom, holding up a brand-spanking-new camera. "It's a Kodak Beau Brownie I ordered out of the Sears, Roebuck catalogue." Then, to Martha: "How's about taking a picture of Jim and me?"

Tom and I had no sooner positioned ourselves with our arms about one anothers' shoulders than Martha snapped our picture. She was fixing to hand the camera back to Tom when Susan tore it out of her grip and dashed it against the ground.

Tom didn't say a word, just stood there looking down at the busted-up camera like it was his very own child.

That afternoon, he went on a week-long tear.

We didn't see either of the Gilchrists for a long time after that. Then, one morning, I was delivering produce to Cedar Key when I run across Tom.

After we had done greeting one another, he reached in his jacket pocket and took out the photograph of him and me at the picnic.

He handed it over.

"Luckily, I was able to salvage this."

"How's the guiding business?"

"Not bad. Not bad atall. Won't be long till I've saved up enough money to buy me another Beau Brownie." Then, sensing my unasked question: "Susan is as churchy as ever. She's taking in sewing and is sending her earnings to a Baptist mission over in Africa."

"Whatever put that notion in her head?"

Tom let out a long, low laugh. "She seen a photograph of it in the Baptist Digest."

6

Pink Cadillac

essie Star used to take in white folks' washing. She was a tall, thin, brown-skinned woman. Rumor had it she had been knocked up by a prominent Levy County white man. At any rate, her son—Willie—was as close to white as you can get and still be colored.

One morning, Bessie was in the kitchen visiting with Mother when we heard a sqawking commotion out back. When I stepped outside, Willie was down on the ground wrestling with a rooster. I separated them and drug Willie into the house.

"What in de world done got aholt of you boy?" screeched Bessie when she spotted his bloody shirt.

I described the scene with the rooster, while Mother ran off to fetch Mercurochrome and bandages.

"Lord have mercy!" exclaimed Bessie. Then, to Willie: "What ails you, chile?"

Willie didn't say a word. He just stood there with a blank expression, staring down at his bare feet.

"Take off your shirt, Willie," said Mother when she returned.

Willie did as told, and Mother covered the scratches on his chest with Mercurochrome.

"Cry, boy!" said Bessie. "Miz Turner and Jim, they won't mind none if you cries."

But Willie refused to shed a tear.

"I swear fo' de Good Lord, something 'bout dat chile ain't natural."

Twenty years passed before next I laid eyes on Willie. In the meantime, I had been elected High-Sheriff of Levy County. I was sitting in the office one evening when I got a phone call from a man in the turpentine business.

"There's a 'sweetback' nigger to the 'quarters' relieving my boys of their hard-earned payday."

"I'm on my way."

When I got there, a new-model pink Cadillac was parked in front of one of the tumbledown shacks. I eased the patrol car in behind it and killed the engine. Blackjack in hand, I walked up to the entrance and pounded on the splintered wooden door.

"Open up in the name of the law!"

I kicked open the door and stepped inside. Kneeling in a frozen circle around a pair of dice were a dozen or so money-fisted Negroes. A nattily attired mulatto stood up to greet me.

"Evening, Sheriff Jim."

It didn't take but a second for me to recognize Willie.

"Well, if it ain't little Willie Star growed tall. Yo' mama tole us you had done moved up to Chicago."

"I was there for a spell, but the weather didn't suit me."

"Something must have suited you to judge by the car you're driving."

"Oh, that . . . That was a gift from a high yeller gal I knows."

"She must be one friendly gal."

Willie bared his teeth in a grin.

"She are that."

Willie was fined five hundred dollars and sentenced to thirty days on the county work farm for running a gambling operation. On his release, he drove to Gainesville in that pink Cadillac of his and started up a cathouse.

Judging by all reports, he was doing pretty good for hisself. Then, a customer got his throat cut by a high-spirited whore, and the authorities were forced to shut the place down.

After that, Willie moved back to Levy County and began running Bolita—a numbers game being broadcast over a Havana radio station.

I knew Willie was operating out of his car, but I couldn't prove it. Finally, in desperation, I told my deputy to stop and search Willie's car anytime he happened to spot it—day or night.

"Shouldn't be hard to spot. It's the only pink Cadillac in the entire of Levy County."

Sure enough, a month later, the deputy found fourteen hundred dollars in cash, along with the payout slips, in the glove compartment.

On the day of the trial, Judge Harlan Murphy—just retired—called me before the bench.

"Sheriff Turner, attorney Milburn here claims his client has been harrassed promiscuously by you and your deputy. 'Cording to him, y'all searched Mr. Star's car well nigh a hundred times without benefit of a search warrant. Is that true?"

"I didn't have time to get a search warrant, Judge. Sometimes, we searched Mr. Star's car three, four times a day."

Judge Murphy cleared his throat and said, "Mr. Sheriff, if you knew for a fact that Mr. Star was in this business, you should have obtained a search warrant. As it stands, I'm afraid I'll have to ask you to return Mr. Star's money, along with the payout slips. Case dismissed."

It didn't take a genius to know something wasn't right. But, given the judge's involvement, there wasn't much I could do about it.

On the way out of the courthouse, I sidled up to Willie and said, "Well, Willie, you fooled us this time, but someday you're gonna get caught."

Willie grinned to beat the band.

"Not me, Mr. Sheriff, sir . . . I'se done learnt my lesson."

For awhile, it looked as though Willie had been telling the truth. Then, one evening, I was working late in the office when the phone rang. It was Floyd Kramer, my deputy to Williston.

"There's been a cutting to colored town, Sheriff Jim. One fella caught t'other in bed with his gal and lopped off his balls and dagger with a knife! I'm at the hospital with the castrated fella now."

"I'll be there directly."

By the time I arrived, the wounded man had died.

"Got any ideas who might have done it?" I asked my deputy.

"A neighbor spotted Willie Star's Cadillac parked out front earlier in the evening."

"Is he sure it was Willie?"

"Ain't but one pink Cadillac in Levy County."

"That don't mean Willie was driving it. What does the girl have to say?"

"I ain't had a chance to question her yet."

"Times awasting!"

Only, when we found the girl, she wouldn't talk.

"Was it Willie Star?" I asked.

"Naw, sir, wasn't Willie."

"Who was it then?"

Silence . . .

"You'll have to tell eventually. Else, you'll be held in contempt of court and sentenced to a prison term."

More silence . . .

I took hold of my deputy's arm.

"C'mon, let's see what you and me can dig up."

But I didn't spend much time pursuing the investigation. 'Cause, early the next morning, an anonymous caller phoned in and said I would find the murderer floating face-up in Fanning Springs. I phoned O.B. Emerson—the Negro undertaker—and told him to meet me there.

O.B. was standing beside the Springs when I arrived.

"Morning, Sheriff Jim," he said in his deep bass voice.

"Morning, O.B. Let's us see if we cain't drum you up a little business."

After we had located the body and drug it to shore, my deputy went and fetched our witness.

"Is this the one done the cutting?" I asked when she had examined the body.

She nodded and I had my deputy drive her on home. Then, I turned the corpse over to O.B. so he could perform an on-the-spot autopsy.

O.B. pointed to what appeared to be a bullet wound.

"See this here hole behind his left ear, Sheriff Jim. This here hole was made with a .38 special, I believe."

"Didn't I hear you say something earlier about wanting to be in charge of the funeral arrangements, O.B.?"

"Yessir, I did."

"Then, you hush up about that there bullet wound. Far as I'm concerned cause of death should be listed as 'accidental drowning.' A suicide, most likely."

"Whatever you say, Sheriff Jim."

Willie stayed out of trouble after that. Oh, he opened a little jook outside Chiefland where an occasional cutting might take place, but that was about it.

A year or so later, I ran into him outside the post office.

"Whatever happened to that pink Cadillac of yours, Willie?"

"Somebody took it, Sheriff Jim."

"Funny, I don't recollect its being reported as stolen."

"Oh, he paid for it later."

"You don't say. How much was it worth to him?"

Willie grinned that shit-eating grin of his.

"Everthin' he had, Sheriff Jim. Everythin' he had."

7

Jim

I t was the fall of '40, and I had just been elected to my first term as High-Sheriff of Levy County. Things were quiet around the office, and I was getting ready to call it a day when the phone rang.

"Sorry to bother you this late of an evening, Sheriff Turner. But, this is Festus Whitfield, and there's a prowler to my house."

Festus was waiting on his front porch when I arrived. I got out of the car—with my bloodhound on a leash—and walked up to him.

"This here is Ears, Festus."

I indicated the dog.

"Just point to where you seen the prowler, and Ears will take her from there."

Festus led us around the corner of the house to the kitchen window.

"My wife was cooking dinner when she seen a hand reach up and snatch a plate of fried chicken off the windowsill."

He had no sooner spoke the words than Ears begun straining on his leash.

"Follow me," I said.

We took off at a trot through the woods—with Ears leading the way. Eventually, we come to a clearing. A boy was setting at the edge of the clearing, polishing off the plate of chicken. He looked familiar, but I didn't recollect ever having seen him before. I handed Festus Ears's leash and walked over.

"What's your name, son?"

"Jim."

I held out my hand.

"Pleased to meet you, Jim."

Martha had dinner waiting on us when we got to the house.

"Martha, this is Jim; Jim, this here is my wife—Martha."

"Pleased to meet you, ma'am."

"Reckon you might could stand a little more fried chicken?" I asked.

"Yes sir, reckon I could."

And he wasn't lying, neither. By the time we were done, he had polished off pretty nigh another whole chicken.

"There's peach cobbler for dessert if you're still hungry," said Martha.

Might as well have asked a Roman lion if he had room for another Christian or two.

"When was the last time you ate, son?" I asked when he come up for air. "Not counting this evening, of course."

"I can't rightly recollect."

"That's a powerful long time. Where's yo' mama and daddy?"

Silence . . .

"Were they mistreating you, boy?" asked Martha.

"No'um, it weren't that exactly. May I be excused now?"

" 'Course, you may. Your room is at the head of the stairs."

"Notice anything peculiar about that boy?" asked Martha when Jim had gone to bed.

"Nothing I can quite put my finger on."

"He's the spitting image of your old girlfriend—Paula Dugan."

When I waked up the next morning, Jim was down in the kitchen waiting on me.

"Don't let her take me back!" he begged.

"I've got no choice, son. Not if she's your legal guardian."

"But you're a Sheriff. Sheriffs can do anything."

"I only wisht that were so. There'd be a whole heap o' changes I'd make in this here world if it were."

"See if you can't run down a 'missing persons' on that 'ere boy I brung in yesterday," I instructed my deputy when I got to work.

I closed the door to my office and brung out the bottle of Canadian Club I kept in my desk drawer for emergencies. I poured some in a glass and thought back on Paula Dugan. . . .

Martha was right. Young Jim could've been Paula's twin brother. Or our son.

"We got something on the boy," said my deputy, interrupting my reverie. "His name is Jim Mills, and he lives with his grandmother to Palatka."

It was late afternoon by the time I arrived at the address the deputy gave me. Getting out of the car, I walked up to the front porch. An elderly lady was setting in a rocker knitting a sweater.

I tipped my hat.

"Afternoon, ma'am."

The lady reluctantly put down her knitting.

"It's about Jim, I suppose. I swear 'fore goodness that chile is gonna be the death of me yet!"

"Gives you a mite of trouble, does he?"

"A mite? I wisht it were only a mite. But then, it's like the Good Book says: 'The trials of the just are many and various'."

I couldn't recall any such quote in the Bible, but I could see Jim had a hard row to hoe at home.

"Mind if I ask a few questions?"

"Ask away. . . . Don't mean I'll answer 'em."

"Who's the child's father?"

"My son, James."

"Mother?"

"That woman's name will never be spoke in this house—not whilst I'm breathing."

"Wouldn't happen to be Paula, would it?"

You could tell by the look on her face I had struck a nerve.

"Maybe; maybe not. Anyway, they're both of 'em dead. Died in a car crash a coupla months after Jim was birthed, and I was stuck with the burden of raising the child."

My next stop was the Putnam County Courthouse. Sure enough, when I checked their records, I found a birth certificate for one James Mills—son of James and Paula—born May 8, 1923. 'Cording to my calculations, that could have made him my son. Then again, he could've been the offspring of James Mills.

Back at the office, there was a message on my desk that read "Call Mrs. Turner. It's urgent."

When I dialed the number, nobody answered.

I got in the patrol car and switched on the siren. I was halfway home when I seen the smoke rising in the distance. By the time I arrived, the volunteer fire department had put out the fire.

"What happened?" I asked Martha when they left.

"I'm not sure, but I think it was young Jim started it. One minute, he was screaming and cursing about you sending him back to that guardian of his. And the next thing I knew, the house was afire."

I recalled the scene in the kitchen that morning. Had I handled things differently, Jim might still be around.

When I phoned Mrs. Mills and told her what had happened, she didn't sound the least bit surprised.

"I suppose he'll be sent to reform school now. But then, it's like the Good Book says: 'The way of the transgressor is hard'."

The next morning, I drove back to Palatka. When I got to the house, Mrs. Mills was setting in the same rocker knitting.

"Did you run him down yet, Sheriff," she asked when she seen me.

"No'um, I ain't." Then, following a pause: "There's one thing I'm curious about though. Who do you reckon it was told Jim about me?"

Silence . . .

"I figured as much."

I turned and headed back toward the car.

"Hold up a minute, Sheriff." Then, when I turned back around: "Do you think it was wrong of me to tell the boy his mother was a Jezebel?"

"When exactly did you tell him?"

"The day before he run away."

Without so much as another word, I got in the car and started up the engine. I turned on the police radio and tried not to think.

We never found Jim.

8

High-Sheriff Jim Turner

Two federal boys were waiting at the farm when I come home from work. I could tell by their expressions they had bad news, but wasn't either of them too quick about spilling it.

Finally, I says, "Boys, I know this here ain't no social visit. Now, what exactly is on your minds?"

"It's about a still," says the one named Bob.

"A still?"

I don't mind admitting I was plenty relieved, having figured it was some damn fool Civil Rights worker done got hisself kilt or some such.

"Reckon it won't be the first time a still's turned up in Levy County, nor the last either."

"This still's different, Jim," said Bob. "This here still was found on your property."

Well sir, I could have swallowed my teeth.

"You sure?"

"Wouldn't hardly be here if we wasn't. It's over to the north pasture, close by Tee Cannon's place."

Tee was one of my colored sharecroppers.

"Well, let's go have a look at her," says I.

We got in the federal boys' cream-colored Ford sedan and drove over to where the still was hid 'midst a copse of palmettos.

"It's a still, all right," I admitted when we was standing next to it.

"It is that," agreed Bob.

"Mind if I nose around a little?"

"'Course not."

I shoved the barrel over some, and the grass underneath was just as green as can be. It hadn't dried out, or blanched, or anything. So I knew that still hadn't been sitting there more than twenty-four hours.

"Reckon it's time we paid Tee a visit," says I.

We drove on back to Tee's house, and I called him out in the front yard.

"You wouldn't happen to know anything about a still over to the north pasture, would you, Tee?"

"Still?" says Tee like he had never heard of any such a thing and wondered what one could be.

"You heard me."

Then, I told him where the still was.

"Well, I swan. I pass that way least once a day. If I'd of knowed a still was nearby, I'd have fetched me home some buck."

"This here ain't no laughing matter, Tee. These are federal boys, and they done found theirselves a still in the High-Sheriff of Levy County's back yard, so to speak."

"I don't know nothing about it, Sheriff Jim. I'd tell you if I did."

I reckon you seen one man lie, you seen 'em all. And Tee wasn't lying. But try and convince the federal boys of that. Nothing would do but Tee accompany them to Ocala that very instant and have his fingerprints took.

"Fine with me," allowed Tee. "So long as the United States government is footing the gas."

The federal boys dropped me off at home, then drove to Ocala with Tee.

I don't mind admitting I was plenty worried. A year earlier, the sheriff before me—Red Loggins—had been sentenced to four years in the federal pen for being in cahoots with the moonshiners. And much as I might have enjoyed the time off, I didn't relish spending it behind bars.

Old Man Charlie Calloway's funeral was the next afternoon, and I was one of the pallbearers. When the graveside service was over, Judge Harlan Murphy—just retired—called me over.

"I believe I know where you can get some information on that still, Jim."

Less than twenty-four hours had passed since they discovered the still on my property, and already the news had spread like wildfire.

"I'd be mighty obliged if you was to let me in on the secret, Judge."

"Morris Sutton. That's your man. Sutton knows everything there is to know about stills. And more besides. He'll tell you where that still come from. But first let me call and tell him you're coming. Otherwise, he'll think you're there to arrest him."

I waited at the courthouse, while the judge phoned Sutton.

"You know where to find him, don't you, Jim?" asked the judge, stepping out of his office.

"Yes sir, I reckon I do."

The judge smiled. "Don't let that make you feel 'shamed. Ain't hardly a growed-up male in the county who hasn't paid Sutton a visit at one time or another."

When I got to Sutton's place, he was setting o/ the front porch just about as full of moonshine whisk as a fellow can be and still be sociable.

"How do, Sheriff. Hear tell you may be *i* market for a still."

"No, sir, done already found one. Only trouble is I don't know who to thank for leaving it on my farm thataway."

"And you reckon I might can help you?"

"That's the story I got from Judge Murphy."

"Reckon I don't owe Judge Murphy no favors!"

Sutton ejected a long, lazy stream of tobacco juice.

"Not after that last one."

"Well, if that's the way it is . . ."

I turned and headed back toward the patrol car.

"Hold your horses a second, Sheriff! Maybe you and me can work something out."

I froze in my tracks with one hand about the door handle.

"Maybe . . ."

"What's it worth? This here information."

"It's worth your not getting arrested for attempting to bribe an officer of the law."

"What's that again?"

"You heared me."

"Judge Murphy claimed you was only coming around for information. Otherwise, I would never have agreed to talk with you."

"Judge Murphy was wrong. It don't happen often. But it happens often enough to make things interesting."

"Well, I'll be . . ."

"Damned," says I.

After that, Sutton got in the car, and we drove over to where the still was.

"Well?" says I when we were standing next to her.

"Ain't never seed one like this before."

But I knew from the way he said it he was lying.

"You sure?"

"Positive."

"This here still wouldn't happen to belong to Jess Dixon, would it?"

Jess had served as deputy under Red Loggins until Loggins was sent to prison and I was appointed to finish out his term.

"Damned if I know."

But he knew, all right.

"I know good'n' well Jess bought it off you. I just want to hear you say it."

Well sir, that done it. Sutton opened up like a Baptist sinner come Judgment Day.

"Honest to God, Sheriff Jim . . . I had no earthly idee them boys was gonna take and plant this still on your farm."

"What boys?"

"Jess Dixon, Ray Burnett, Flavis Gerald, and Brian Lyn. That's who. I bought it off a fella to Ocala for two hundred and seventy-five dollars, and them boys give me four hundred dollars cash money. But, honest to God, Sheriff Jim, I didn't know nothing 'bout what they had in mind. Else, I'd never have sold her."

I wrapped my arm about his shoulders all friendly-like.

"I believe you, Morris. But I'll need you to repeat what you just said to the federal boys."

"Whatever you say, Sheriff Jim."

So I carried Sutton to Bronson and locked him up in a cell for safekeeping until I could contact the federal boys.

The next morning, I phoned Ocala and told them what Sutton had told me the day before. Then, I and my deputy rounded up the four suspects. Burnett, Gerald, and Lyn were rumored to be big in 'shine, and—like I said—Dixon had been the former deputy under Red Loggins. I put the prisoners in seperate cells so they couldn't talk to one another, then waited for the federal boys to arrive.

"I reckon you'll be some pleased to know your sharecropper, Tee Cannon, has a clean record," said Bob after we shook hands.

"Don't surprise me the least little bit."

"Where's the suspects?" asked the one whose name I can't recall.

"In separate cells, cooling their heels till you boys could get here."

"Well, bring 'em down one at a time, and we'll question 'em each one separate."

I brought Jess Dixon down first. Jess, he was smart. He didn't know nothing about a still, had never seen one.

"Is it true you been petitioning Governor Philpot to have yourself appointed sheriff?" I asked.

"So what if it is? Ain't no law against that I know of."

"No, sir, there ain't. I was just curious. That's all."

After that, Jess shut up tight as a clam and demanded to see his lawyer. So I led him back to his cell and brung down Ray Burnett.

Ray, he was as smart as Jess. If not smarter. To listen at him talk, you'd swear he had never had a taste of 'shine in his life.

Finally, Bob says, "Bring down Sutton. He's the man we need to see."

So I went and fetched Sutton.

"Honest to God, I done told you everything I know, Sheriff Jim!" says he on the way to my office.

"I know you did, Morris. But it's high time them federal boys was let in on the secret."

"But, Sheriff Jim—"

"No 'buts' about it. My ass is in a sling, and you're the onliest one can get me out."

I left Sutton outside my office with the deputy and went in alone. The federal boys were starting to grow impatient.

"This had better be good, Sheriff," growled the one. "Otherwise, we're liable to think you're grasping at straws."

"Go ahead and bring him in, Jim," says Bob. "Maybe he's the key to this whole mess."

So I brung in Sutton.

"Mr. Sutton, do you know anything about a still that was found on Sheriff Turner's place?" asked Bob, all official-like.

"I ain't too sure."

"Sutton—" I says.

"Don't go intimidating the witness, Jim," warned Bob. "Else, we'll have to ask you to leave the room."

"Just tell them what you told me yesterday, Morris."

"You heard the sheriff," seconded Bob.

"I need me a goddamned drink of whiskey, Sheriff," says Sutton, nervous-like.

"Is that all right with you all?" I asked the federal boys.

"W-w-well, it's highly irregular. . . ." stammered the one.

"Go ahead," said Bob, giving his partner a dirty look.

The "evidence" room, where we stored confiscated moonshine, was across the hall from my office. I led Sutton over and unlocked the door. I flicked on the light.

"Make yourself to home. I'll be back to fetch you in half an hour."

Well, that made a friend out of Sutton. When he come back in, he told the federal boys everything he had told me the day before. And more besides. Then, I brung the suspects down one at a time, and Sutton repeated for their benefit what he had told us.

Finally, Brian Lyn broke down and confessed. Said it had all been a scheme to run me out of office so they could get their own man—Jess Dixon—in.

After that, the federal boys wanted to drive Sutton home. But Sutton was in no hurry to leave.

"I'd be mighty obliged if you was to let me back in the 'evidence' room, Sheriff Jim," says he, all polite-like.

"Here's the key. You drink as much as you like of whatever you like."

And he did.

9

The Pony

I was sipping a cherry Coke in Henessey's Drugstore when the girl behind the counter went into labor.

"Take her easy, little lady."

I led her out to the patrol car and switched on the siren.

"I'll have you to the hospital in no time."

An hour later, Geneva King was delivered of a seven-pound boy.

"How's Geneva's baby coming along?" asked Martha that evening when I come home.

"Couldn't be better. Why, that there child's got a pair of lungs on him what could outbellow a castrated hog!"

As we were preparing for bed, Martha turned to me and said, "Your daddy says it's not likely we'll ever have children."

" 'Tain't your fault, Honey Lamb. Just weren't in the cards, I reckon."

Martha began to cry.

"Oh, Jim, I want a baby worse than anything in this world." Then, taking hold of my shoulders and looking me square in the eye, "Wish we had one like Geneva's, don't you, Jim Turner?"

The way she said it like to broke my heart.

"Reckon you're all the family I'll need "enduring" this lifetime, Honey Lamb."

Geneva hadn't been out of the hospital a week before her husband up and left her.

"Where do you reckon he run off to?" I asked when she dropped by the office to fill out a "missing persons."

"Don't know and don't care. Me and little Grady will get along just fine without him."

"Maybe I could be of help."

"If you're talking charity, you can just forget it. Ain't nobody in my family ever been on the dole, and I ain't about to be the first."

"I wasn't talking charity. I thought you might could use a baby sitter whilst you're to work, and I got just the candidate."

That evening, over dinner, I broached the subject with Martha.

"Geneva King was by the office today. 'Pears Roy has left for good."

"Good riddance to bad rubbish, says I. But how is Geneva going to support herself and the child?"

"She still has her job to the drugstore, but she'll need someone to look after Grady while she's at work." Then, when Martha didn't say anything: " 'Pears to me like you might welcome a little distraction now you've retired from schoolteaching."

"I might at that."

"You'll do her then?"

"Wouldn't hardly be human if I didn't."

After that, I'd come home of an evening, and it would be Grady this or Grady that. When Grady spoke his first word, there wasn't a prouder "mother" in the entire of Levy County.

"Why, I wouldn't be at all surprised if he grew up to be President of the United States," said Martha.

"Don't you think that might be stretching it a mite?"

I was fond of Grady, but I managed to keep my wits about me.

"Only a mite."

As the years passed, Martha grew more and more attached to the boy. On his sixth birthday, she threw a party and took half the youngsters in Levy County to the circus at Gainesville.

When Grady seen the bareback riders, wouldn't nothing do but he have a horse of his own. So I bought a Shetland pony off Simon Green to Chiefland, and we give it to Grady on his birthday.

After work, I'd drive over to the north pasture. Grady would be circling the field on his pony as Martha watched from a fence post.

"Mind Grady don't become too attached to that animal," I warned. "After all, ponies are delicate creatures. He's liable to catch the hoof-and-mouth and die on us."

"I honestly don't know what would become of Grady if that were to happen. It's like that pony is his own flesh and blood."

Grady hadn't had the pony a year when Geneva remarried and reclaimed her son. Her husband was a nice enough fella what owned a cattle ranch to Williston. Williston weren't no more than half an hour's drive from where we lived at Bronson. But, it might as well have been at the ends of the earth so far as Martha was concerned.

"Reckon he misses me?" she asked, following one of our Sunday visits to Geneva and the boy. "After all, he's got growed-up horses to ride now."

"'Course, he misses you."

"You never could lie worth a damn, Jim Turner!"

After that, I'd come home of an evening, and Martha would be keeping steady company with a bottle.

"What's ailing you, Honey Lamb," I asked finally.

"You know good and well what's ailing me, Jim Turner! And it's gonna keep right on ailing me till the day I die."

"Lord knows, there's plenty of childless couples on this here earth 'sides us."

"That doesn't make it any easier to bear."

"No sir, I reckon it don't."

Things went from bad to worser after that.

One evening, I come home from work and found a note on the kitchen table.

"Gone to Williston," was all it said.

When I got to the ranch, Geneva and her husband were standing in the driveway. "She's inside with Grady," said Geneva. Then, before I could enter: "It ain't the first time she's driven out alone thisaway, Sheriff Jim."

Back at the house, Martha was fit to be tied.

"What do you mean busting in on Grady and me when we were fixing to go riding?"

"The boy don't belong to you, Honey Lamb. He belongs to Geneva and her husband. 'Sides, Grady ain't the onliest child in the world. There's plenty of unwanted chillun to choose from."

"Maybe, you're right. It isn't like it used to be. Grady's glad to see me right enough, but it isn't as though he couldn't live without me. Still, can't anybody take his place."

"But—"

"But, nothing. Out of the kitchen now. I've got work to do."

Wasn't too many days later Geneva called me at the office.

"Grady's disappeared. One instant, he was out in the front yard playing; the next, he had vanished."

"Did you try Martha at the house?"

"Wasn't any answer."

"Mind if I hold off an hour or so before putting in an 'all points.' I've got a pretty good idea where they are."

"Whatever you think best, Sheriff Jim."

Martha was setting on the fence post watching Grady circle the pasture on his pony when I eased up behind her in the truck and got out.

"Boy's a pretty fair country rider!"

"Fair, you say! Why, Jim Turner, you know good and well he's a Class A world beater!"

I walked over and took hold of Martha's hand.

"Whatever you say, Honey Lamb." Then: "Geneva's worried sick. She didn't know where the two of you run off to. Don't you think you oughta tell her the next time?"

"Won't be any next time. I suppose you've come to take him back?"

I nodded.

"It's just as well. Geneva's a good mother."

I didn't have an answer for that one.

"Hold me, Jim Turner," said Martha.

I took her in my arms, and we held on to one another for what seemed an eternity. Then, I rounded up the pony, and the three of us got in the truck and drove back to Williston.

A month later, the pony took sick and died.

10

A Fallen Sparrow

It was a Sunday morning, and I was out in the front yard washing my patrol car when a message come in over the radio.

"Calling Sheriff Turner . . . Calling Sheriff Turner . . . Come in, Sheriff Turner."

I reached in the car window and lifted the receiver.

"This here is Sheriff Turner. What seems to be the problem?"

"There's been a homicide over to Dixie County, and Sheriff Mark Bone's done been kilt."

"What's that you say?"

"Homer Sudlow done kilt Sheriff Bone. First off, he shot a man name of Amos Andrews. Then, when Sheriff Bone went to fetch him in, he kilt him too."

"Where's Homer now?"

"Holed up in his house with the entire of the Dixie County police force out in his front yard."

The Dixie County police force consisted of two part-time deputies.

"Tell 'em to hold their horses! I'll be there directly."

I got in my car and drove out to Sudlow's house. When I arrived, the two deputies were crouched down behind their patrol car. I joined them.

"Where's Sheriff Bone?"

The senior of the two pointed his .38 in the direction of the front porch where Bone's body lay spread-eagle before the door.

"Single blast from a double-aught done it."

"How's it going with Homer?"

"Not so good."

"Maybe we ought to bring his wife around."

I got on the radio and asked the dispatch at the Dixie County courthouse to put Mrs. Sudlow on the line.

"You willing to try and talk your husband in?"

"Anything you say, Sheriff Jim."

Wasn't long after that a beat-up Chevy truck rounded the curve and rolled to a stop within a few yards of us. The door swung open, and out stepped the prettiest female woman I ever laid eyes on.

Without so much as a glance in our direction, she cupped her hands about her mouth and screamed, "Homer Sudlow, you come out here this instant! You hear me?"

"Now, Maggie . . ." replied a trembling voice from in the house.

"Don't you 'Now, Maggie' me, Homer."

Mrs. Sudlow stalked off in the direction of the house.

"I won't stand for it."

"Mrs. Sudlow, you can't go in there," I hollered after her.

But she was already halfway home.

"Are you gonna come out peaceable-like, Homer? Or am I gonna have to drag you out?"

She had no sooner spoke the magic words than the front door swung open and out stepped Homer—sans shotgun.

"Put your hands behind your head, Homer," I commanded, standing up straight and pointing my .38 at his heart.

Homer did as he was told and stepped out in the yard.

"Cuff him," I said to the senior of the two deputies.

That evening, I was setting in the living room reading the paper when there come a knock on the door. When I opened it, Mrs. Sudlow was standing on the stoop.

"May I come in, Sheriff?"

"Course, you can."

I waved her inside. Then, when she was seated on the couch and I had taken the chair opposite: "What exactly is on your mind, Mrs. Sudlow?"

"It's about Homer. He's innocent, you know."

"In the case of Sheriff Bone, there's two Dixie County deputies what'll swear otherwise. As for the earlier homicide, you yourself admitted he done that one."

"Oh, Homer pulled the trigger, all right. Still, it weren't all his fault. Not by a long shot."

It was then Mrs. Sudlow told me her story. Seems Homer had gotten drunk at one of the jooks to Old Town and was driving home in his truck when Sheriff Bone pulled him over. A brief tussle ensued, and Homer wound up charged with D.W.I. and resisting arrest.

Bone took Homer to the jail at Old Town and locked him up. Then, he phoned Amos Andrews—the local bail bondsman. Homer didn't have a pot to piss in, much less the thousand dollars he needed to go his bail. So when Andrews arrived, he signed over the deed to his farm as collateral.

The next morning, when he was sober, Homer realized what he had done. But it was too late. If he didn't come up with a thousand dollars cash money by the end of the month, the farm would belong to Andrews.

When Mrs. Sudlow come to this point in her story, she hesitated.

"Don't know if I can tell the rest . . ."

"Reckon I already know."

"I only done it to save the farm."

"D'ya think Sheriff Bone was in cahoots with this here bail bondsman fella?"

"I wouldn't doubt it."

"Well, let me nose around some and see what I can come up with."

The next morning, I called on a Negro I knowed who run a jook to Dixie County.

"Ever had any dealings with a bail bondsman by the name of Andrews, Willie?"

According to Willie, Andrews was lowdown as a snake and twice as slippery. It was his practice to bail the local coloreds out of jail for some minor offense, then charge 'em two, three dollars a month interest. Till, in some cases, the original fine had done been paid a hundred times over.

"Was Sheriff Bone a party to this?"

"Wouldn't swear to it . . . But it's a true fact I've been paying Sheriff Bone 'under the table' money all these many years to keep him from shutting down my jook."

On the afternoon of his trial, I was transporting Homer to the Dixie County Courthouse when we come to the cemetery where Sheriff Bone was buried. I turned at the entrance and pulled up alongside Bone's grave. Getting out of the car, I swung open the back door and motioned for Homer to join me.

"Let's you and me get out and pay our respects."

Even if Bone had been a crook, I felt like he deserved that much. After all, he had been a sheriff.

Homer got out of the car, his hands cuffed behind his back, and we walked up to the grave together. I was fixing to say a short prayer when I felt a tug at my holster. The next thing I knowed, Homer had aholt of my .38 and was aiming it at my heart.

"How in tarnation!"

Then, I seen the chain connecting his cuffs had been cut in two.

"Where'd you get the file, Homer?"

"Never you mind about that! Just hand over the keys to your car."

It was then I told him what I had uncovered about Andrews and Sheriff Bone.

"If you'll give me back my gun, we'll pretend none of this ever happened."

"Its too late for that now, Sheriff. Hand over the keys, or else."

I handed over the keys.

Homer was long gone by the time my deputy found me cuffed to the chainlink fence surrounding the cemetery.

"How'd he get the drop on you, Sheriff Jim?"

"Never you mind about that. Just get behind the wheel of the car and follow my directions. Homer ain't likely to leave that pretty wife of his behind."

Sure enough, the patrol car was parked alongside Homer's truck in the front yard of his house when we arrived.

I told the deputy to pull up alongside her, then stepped out of the car with my double-aught.

"We know you're in there, Homer. Come on out with your hands up, and I'll see you're given a fair trial."

I had no sooner spoke the words than the front door swung open and out stepped Homer with my gun in his hand. I squeezed back on both triggers of the double-aught, and Homer slammed over backwards on the porch with a sickening thud.

"You've done kilt him!"

Mrs. Sudlow rushed out of the house and knelt beside his body.

"What'd you want to go and do that for? He wasn't going to hurt nobody. He'd had enough of killing."

"It was him or me, Mrs. Sudlow."

Mrs. Sudlow lifted Homer's head and placed it gently in her lap. "The gun wasn't even loaded. Homer removed the bullets before y'all arrived."

I walked over and lifted the revolver. Sure enough, when I flipped open the cylinder, the chamber was empty.

Mrs. Sudlow began crying.

"I told him he shouldn't have come back for me. But then, Homer always was a fool where I was concerned."

"Was Mrs. Sudlow toting her purse when she visited the prisoner this morning?" I asked my deputy when we were back to the station filling out forms.

"Yessir, she was. Why?"

"No reason. Just curious. That's all."

"You never did explain how Homer got shy of them cuffs, Sheriff Jim?"

"He wrestled my gun away and forced me to clip the chain with them there metal cutters from inside the trunk."

"Wrestled your gun away! With his hands cuffed behind his back?"

"You heared me. Hesh up now so's we can get this here paperwork done before next month rolls around."

11

An Old Hound

Most nights, since I retired from sheriffing, I sit out on the back porch and watch the boats moving past on the Suwanee River. Here, at Fowler's Bluff, we're no more than a stone's throw from the Gulf of Mexico. Back in the old days, before the old ticker commenced acting up, I used to spend a lot of time fishing and clamming in the waters hereabouts, but now I mostly just sit and watch. Some nights, two dozen or more boats go by during the course of an evening. Over the last few years, a goodly number of those boats have been loaded with marijuana. You can tell by the way their gunnels sit close by the water as though they were carrying a heavy load, and the fact they seldom if ever use running lights.

One night, Tom Gilchrist from down the river was by the house visiting when one of the marijuana boats went past. When I pointed it out, he told me a story.

Seems he and another old boy were out night fishing by Shell Mound the week before when the biggest airboat either of them ever laid eyes on roared past and pulled up to the landing. A pickup with a camper body was backed up waiting, and those boys couldn't count the number of bales loaded on that trailer. When the fellows in the airboat were done, the driver of the truck cranked her up and headed down the dirt road with the headlights switched off.

The airboat swung around to the county boat ramp on the opposite shore, and another pickup with a boat trailer attached backed down to where they could load up the boat. The two fellows from the airboat jumped into the cab alongside the driver, and they drove off.

"What d'ya think of that, Brother Jim?" asked Tom when he had done with his story.

"Hell, you shoulda spoke up and made yourself known. That way, them marijuana people would've had to pay you around twenty-five thousand apiece to keep your mouths shut. Either that, or kilt you. Whichever was easiest."

Well, Tom didn't think that was funny, and I can't say I blame him. It's a crying shame when a fellow can't go night fishing without taking his life in his hands. But then, that's always been the case around these parts. Back in the twenties and early thirties, it was bootleg whiskey: in the fifties and sixties, it was moonshine.

Ray Burnett—the biggest producer of white lightning in the county—used to bring in a semitrailer of sugar from Jacksonville, then load up the same trailer with moonshine to sell on the way back. Red Loggins—our high-sheriff for a brief stretch in the early fifties—was mixed up with Burnett until the federal boys gathered enough evidence to have him shipped off to the federal pen at Atlanta. But that's a whole 'nother story.

The morning after Tom's visit, I decided to pay a call on our present high-sheriff—Malcolm Bly. I climbed in the Ford and drove over to the brand-spanking-new courthouse at Bronson. When I entered Bly's office, a pretty little receptionist told me to have a seat, the sheriff would be with me in a minute. Well sir, that minute extended itself to a half-hour, and then that half-hour extended itself to a whole one. By the time I was finally ushered into the high-sheriff's inner sanctum, I had done reading a *True Detective* and a *Reader's Digest* and had started in on a *Farmer's Life*.

Sheriff Bly stood up from his desk and held out his hand when I entered.

"What'd you want to see me about, Sheriff Jim?"

I didn't mince words.

"It's about them marijuana boats."

"Marijuana boats?" echoed he increduously, like he had never heared of any such athing.

"Mar-i-jua-na boats," I enunciated slowly and evenly so there was no mistaking my drift. "The ones what pass by my back porch of an evening."

"Talk to the conservation boys. They're the ones in charge of curtailing that sort of activity these days."

"Conservation boys? I never heared tell of them being in charge of no 'square grouper' before. I had always reckoned their jurisdiction not to extend beyond the flesh-and-blood kind."

"There's been a change in policy since the days when you were sheriffing, Jim."

"I'll say there has. Back when I was sheriffing, it was only the colored smoked marijuana, and not many of them. Leastways, not enough to keep a dozen or more boats loaded up and moving down the Suwanee River of an evening."

"Times change. . . ."

"You can say that again. In my day, the High-Sheriff of Levy County didn't average more'n ten, twelve thousand dollars a year. Today, it must be closer to two hundred thousand!"

"What d'ya mean by that?"

It was then I laid my trump card on him.

"I was referring to that new house of yours. Judging from the outside of it, I'd guesstimate it cost you close by a quarter of a million United States dollars to build."

Sheriff Bly grinned sheepishly.

"Got me a home loan. . . ."

"Is that so? To look at her, you'd never guess that place was intended to be a farmhouse. Was the pool covered by the loan, too, or was that extry?"

Sheriff Bly commenced shuffling some official-looking papers laying on his desk.

"If you'll excuse me, Jim, I have to be getting back to work."

"Whatever you say, Sheriff. I realize you're an awfully busy man. Me, on the other hand, I got nothing to do of an evening but sit out on my back porch and watch the marijuana boats go past."

Well, you could tell by Bly's worried expression I had shook him some. So I took that opportunity to mosey on out of there—figuring to maybe do a little missionary work on my own.

The first thing I done was to pay Tom Gilchrist a visit to see about borrowing his boat. I had sold mine two years before when I decided I was getting too old and feeble to be going out on the river, much less the Gulf. Taking a boat out is hard work, and these old bones just weren't up to it. But this here was different. If I didn't follow up the trail now, it would be like turning a hound loose on a scent, then commanding him to heel. I couldn't let go this thing now if my life depended on it. In a manner of speaking, it did because the word was these marijuana people weren't the sort to mess with—not and continue breathing.

Tom loaned me his skiff, and that evening, 'stead of watching the boats pass by from the comfort of my back porch, I was out on the river close by Shell Mound shivering and rueing the day I decided to become a lawman. The way I see it, being a lawman is akin to contracting an unknown virus. Once it's entered your bloodstream, there's no way on God's green earth to work your way shy of it. So I just sat in the boat and shivered.

But that wasn't the worst part. As luck would have it, the marijuana boys had decided to take the evening off. So I spent the evening out on the water for nothing.

When I drug myself back home the next morning, I felt as old and tired as I had felt in my life. And that was plenty old and plenty tired. It wasn't until I had poured down four or five cups of scalding black coffee that I begun to feel almost human again and was able to drag my weary carcass back to the bedroom for a much-needed snooze.

Tom came over to my house around five that afternoon with a story to tell. Seems one of Bly's deputies had been by to see him right after I left with the boat. They had chatted about this and that until the deputy managed to bring the conversation around to the skiff—pretending all the while it was my welfare he was concerned with in that a man of my age and physical condition (heart trouble, pleurisy) shouldn't be out on the water alone. Well, his line of questioning didn't fool Tom the least little bit, but he was able to claim quite honestly not to have the slightest notion why I borrowed the boat.

I thanked Tom for coming over to tell me about his conversation with the deputy and invited him to stay for dinner. He accepted my invite, and I fried up a mess of bream an old boy had brought over the day before. After Tom and I had done eating, we took chairs out on the back porch. Sure enough, the fleet of marijuana boats was back in business. The hound being off the scent, so to speak, the hares were having theirselves a field day! Only, I had been a rabbit hound for going on too many years to discourage that easy.

The next morning, I was up early and went out to the boat. It had been cold the night before, and there were patches of frost on the ground. Ever so gently, I eased my old bones into the boat and pull-started the engine. Once I had her going, I puttered down the river toward Shell Mound, casting out lines along the way like I was trolling. The area around Shell Mound was deserted. So I anchored her to the east bank across from the county boat ramp and stepped out on dry land.

The sun had risen quite a bit since I left home, and its feeble warmth helped to invigorate my rusty joints. I walked a ways up the dirt road Tom claimed the truck with the marijuana went down and examined its muddy surface for fresh tire tracks. Sure enough, a truck with a semitrailer had passed by the night before.

So they haven't altered the procedure the least little bit, I thought. Reckon they figure an old man like myself is easily discouraged. It was then I formulated a plan.

That evening around seven, I got in the Ford and drove out to where the dirt road intersects County Road 345. I parked the car amid a stand of trees to conceal it from anyone driving by and commenced my vigil.

Around eleven, a truck with a semitrailer attached pulled off the highway and headed down the dirt road. Once it was out of sight, I took a roadblock with flashing red neon signals out of my trunk and placed it in the center of the road. Then, for the clincher, I laid a long line of sixteen-penny nails embedded in a broad, flat board underneath.

Sure enough, a half hour later, the truck with my hare come barrelling down the road with its headlights switched off. Without even bothering to apply the brakes, it run smack dab into my snare. There was a sound like twin explosions, and the truck went skittering into the underbrush—leveling two small pines.

"Hold her right there," I shouted, firing several rounds from a .38 police special and a .44 Magnum with heavy loads to make it appear like I was heading up a small army.

Well sir, I needn't have bothered because, as it turned out, the old boy wrestling that semi was too banged up to put up more than token resistance.

By the time he crawled out of the cab, looking hurt and dejected, with a swelled-up face and two black eyes, I had my .38 aimed betwixt his eyeballs.

"Take her nice and easy," I commanded him.

"Why, Sheriff Jim," says he, a suprised look on his face. "What in tarnation has this got to do with you?"

It was Ray Burnett—the former moonshine Kingpin's baby boy, Sonny. No use explaining to him I was doing my duty. Duty meant nothing to him—nor his daddy, either.

"I'd have thought you and your daddy might have learnt your lessons by now, Sonny. 'Specially after your daddy's stretch in the federal pen."

But Sonny wasn't talking.

"Come along then. . . . And help me load one of these here marijuana bales in the trunk of the car to serve as evidence."

Sonny did as told, and we drove back to my house where I put a call through to the federal boys at Ocala. When I told them what had happened, they were only too happy to drive the hundred or so miles to my house and take my deposition before I turned the prisoner over to them for safekeeping.

"Would you like a drink, Sonny?" I asked when I had hung up the receiver. "It's liable to be the last one you'll enjoy for a spell."

Sonny nodded, and I went over to the kitchen counter to mix him a C.C. and Seven.

"How's your daddy doing these days?" I asked after I handed him his drink.

Back in the early fifties, Sonny's father—Ray— had attempted to implicate me in the moonshine business by having a still planted on my farm as evidence for the federal boys to uncover. But, like I said before, that's a whole 'nother story. 'Sides, didn't much come of it.

"He's doing all right," grumbled Sonny.

"Is he mixed up in all this, too? Or is it just you boys and Sheriff Bly?"

Once again, Sonny didn't say a word, but I could tell by the way his eyes lighted up he knew what I was talking about.

"Things would go a lot easier for you if you was to turn state's evidence against Bly."

Well, sir, that done it! Sonny opened up like a Baptist sinner come Judgment Day.

"Honest to God, Sheriff Jim, I was just a poor honest fisherman 'til the day one of Bly's deputies come around and offered me more money than I had ever heard tell of to bring in a load of marijuana."

"I believe you, Sonny. But them federal boys are liable to take some convincing."

"Just tell me how I ought to go about it, Sheriff Jim, and I'll tell 'em everything I know."

Sonny was just an ignorant old country boy, and I knew it. Still, I didn't want to take advantage of the fact—now that I had him cornered. 'Sides, what could it possibly gain me or anyone else to put Sonny behind bars when it was the brains of the operation we were after?

"Don't you go telling those federal boys a thing until after they've granted you a Writ of Immunity. Then, tell 'em everything you know about Sheriff Bly and any other aspects of the operation you know about."

And that was just how it turned out. When the federal boys arrived, I told them all I knew in a deposition, and they carried Sonny back to jail at Ocala. The following morning, Sonny was granted immunity for turning state's evidence against his fellow smugglers—including Sheriff Bly and two of his deputies. Whether or not Sonny's daddy, Ray, was involved I don't know. After all, you can't expect a son to testify against his daddy. But, at any rate, Sheriff Bly became the second High-Sheriff of Levy County in less than thirty years to be sent to the federal pen at Atlanta, and I returned to my nightly vigil on the Suwanee River with a few less marijuana boats to contend with.

Not that I have anything against smoking marijuana, understand. Hell, I'd probably be smoking the stuff myself if I was fifty years younger. But an old hound like myself just naturally follows a trail to its conclusion. Wouldn't hardly be natural if he didn't.

12

Letting Go

In my dream, the hounds are baying something fierce like they've got something treed, and I'm charging lickety-split through the underbrush just as fast as these two old legs will carry me. But, try as I might, I can't catch up to 'em. Not for the life of me! The next thing I know I'm wide awake with light streaming through my bedroom window, and just outside is the Suwanee River moiling its way slowly westward to the Gulf of Mexico.

Well, we've fooled 'em, again. Ain't we, Jim Turner? says I to myself, as, ever so gently, I ease my feet over the edge of the bed and, using my elbows as fulcrums, hoist myself into a sitting position.

Following a light breakfast, I take the Ford and drive into Chiefland. I park the car alongside Main Street and duck around the corner to the barbershop.

"How do, Sheriff Jim," says Curly when I enter.

"How do, Curly," says I for the umpteenth time. "Shave and a trim, please."

I take a seat in the old timey barber chair facing the mirror and stare back at the image of myself, who has become an elderly gentleman.

"Ain't dead yet. Not by a long shot," I say aloud before I can catch myself.

"What's that you say, Jim?"

Curly throws the sheet across my lap and ties the two strings about my neck.

"Oh, nothing. I was just talking to myself. That's all."

That's when Curly gives me the look reserved for old people that says "Dear God in heaven, please don't let him crack up on me now."

"Don't worry none, Curly. I ain't about to start foaming at the mouth. Not yet, anyways."

Curly laughs then like it had been a joke all along.

"That reminds me . . ."

He launches into a story about a mad dog that I know by heart.

"Reckon you could change the ending this time around Curly? The old one's fine, but I could stand a little variety."

At this point, Old Man Andrews enters the shop. Old Man Andrews is no more'n five years my senior, but he looks old enough to have given Methuselah a run for his money.

"How do, Mr. Andrews," Curly greets him.

"Have done better!"

"Well, grab a seat on the bench, and take a load off yo' feet," says Curly, trying to be friendly though you can tell by the edge in his voice it's a strain.

Mr. Andrews leans forward on the bench and squints in my general direction.

"That you, Jim Turner?"

"Yessir, it's me all right."

"How're the bass biting out to your place these days?"

Truth to tell, it's been well nigh six months since the last time I was out on the river, but I ain't about to let Curly and Old Man Andrews in on the secret.

"Tolerably, well, thank you. Caught me a sixteen-pounder t'other day fishing near the north bank."

Curly emits a long low whistle.

"You don't say! That's right smart of a fish."

I can tell by the amused expression on his face Mr. Andrews is on to me.

"A sixteen-pounder, eh? Who did the weighing?"

"Me, of course."

"Jim, if your eyes are anything like mine, that fish might just as well have weighed sixteen hundred pounds for all you would have knowed from looking at the scales."

He has me there. So I close my eyes and lean back in the chair like I'm fixing to doze off.

"Don't try and play possum with me, Jim Turner! I know better!" screams Old Man Andrews, tapping the metal tip of his cane against the tile floor.

"Calm down now, Mr. Andrews," Curly warns him. "Else I'm gonna have to call your wife to come and fetch you."

Old Lady Andrews is even older than her husband, but as full of piss and vinegar as the day she was birthed. A couple of years back, I seen the two of 'em engage in a shouting match, and the old man finished a distant second.

Old Man Andrews holds his tongue till I'm fixing to leave, then says, "Watch out one of them bass don't take and pull you out of that boat of yours, Jim Turner!"

"I'll do that. And you be sure and offer my condolences to Mrs. Andrews for having to put up with an old scoundrel like yourself all these many years."

When I get back to the Ford, a young sheriff's deputy is pasting a parking ticket on the front windshield.

"How do, Sheriff Jim . . . I didn't recognize your automobile. But as you can see, the parking meter's done run out of time."

"Oh, really . . . I could have swore I dropped a quarter in the slot. Must have been a nickel. These old eyes ain't hardly what they used to be."

"Well, I'm awful sorry to have to give you a citation, but you know how it is once the ticket's done been writ up and all."

"I reckon I do at that. Having served five terms as high-sheriff of this here county. But it 'pears to me a young, ambitious fella such as yourself would think twice before posting a parking ticket on a car with a Florida Sheriff's Association sticker on the rear windshield."

I snatch the ticket from underneath the wiper and jam it deep in my pants' pocket. Then, without so much as another word, I get in the Ford and drive home.

Back at the house, I tear the ticket into tiny pieces and toss the pieces into the wastebasket.

Dust to dust. Ashes to ashes.

I fix myself a sausage sandwich and sit down at the kitchen table. I haven't taken the first bite when the phone rings. Rising unsteadily to my feet, I pad over and lift the receiver.

"Hello."

"Is this the Turner residence?"

"It is."

"Is Mrs. Turner in?"

"Mrs. Turner ain't been in for going on ten years now."

There's a slight hesitation before the voice continues.

"Are you the gentleman of the house then?"

"I'm the onliest one who lives here if that's what you mean. But I wouldn't go so far as to call me a gentleman."

"Well, this is Sheila Kay with Pan products . . ."

"Whatever it is you're selling, I ain't buying!"

I slam down the receiver.

Now, what did you want to go and act like that for? I ask myself once I have sat back down. *Girl wasn't doing nothing but her job.*

No longer hungry, I shove the plate aside and wander out to the back porch. Taking a seat on my favorite rocker, I peer out over the river. Suddenly, I'm reminded of something that happened when I was a young'un.

A bunch of us boys were skinny-dipping in the river one afternoon when I got the cramps and went under. The more I struggled, the deeper I sank, until everything was pitch black. Eventually, I ceased struggling, and a funny sort of peace settled over me. Drowning wasn't near as hard as having a tooth pulled, say. Matter of fact, it was downright pleasurable. At that instant, I felt an arm about my neck. The next thing I knew my head broke the surface, and my rescuer—Tom Gilchrist—was treading water alongside of me.

Tom Gilchrist! He died not too long ago, and I served as a pallbearer at his funeral. It's funny his saving my life thataway, then me living long enough to serve as his pallbearer. But, it's like the Good Book says: "The ways of the Lord are passing strange."

Watching the river roll past makes me drowsy, and the next thing I know a series of images is flashing before my eyes.

I'm nine years old and out hunting with Daddy. A coon hound by the name of Ears is chasing a rabbit through the underbrush, while Daddy and I trail along behind.

Paula Dugan and I are setting out on her front porch, and I'm whispering something in her ear. A faint smile lights up Paula's face as she reaches out and takes hold of my hand.

I'm on my lunch break at the sawmill, and Tom Gilchrist and I are setting on a wooden bench with our lunch pails betwixt our legs. Tom manages to get off a good one, and his face creases in an ear-to-ear grin.

My wife, Martha, is standing before the kitchen sink doing the dishes. I walk up behind her and, entwining my arms about her waist, bend over to kiss a soap sud off her cheek.

Cousin Chauncey and I are out on the river fishing for bream. Chauncey has a fifth of George Dickel in one hand and a bottle of Lea & Perrins sauce to chase it with in the other. His cane pole is leaning against the gunnels of the johnboat.

The governor, in the person of Chauncey, is swearing me in for my first term as High-Sheriff of Levy County. I've got my right hand on the Holy Bible, and my left is raised in the air. There's a solemn look on my face.

"I, Jim Turner . . ."

I'm standing over Homer Sudlow's dead body with a smoking shotgun in my hands. *God knows, I'm sorry, Homer. But it was either you or me. And I didn't intend for it to be me. Not this time around.*

I'm retired from sheriffing and living out on the farm with my tenant, Tee Cannon. The two of us are on tractors plowing at opposite ends of a field. Tee looks over in my direction and waves. I wave back.

I'm old and living on the Suwanee River. I walk out on the back porch to watch the river roll past. Daddy and Tom Gilchrist are standing on the opposite shore beckoning for me to join them. When I stand, it's as though I've sloughed off my body and am suddenly young again.

Then, the images fade, and my recurring dream flashes into focus. Only, this time out, my feet are as light as feathers, and I have the strangest feeling I am about to catch up to that pack of baying hounds. . . .

Epilogue

Jim Turner died on February 1, 1987. In March of that year, the Suwanee River overflowed its banks to an extent unparalleled in this century.